This Little Book Belongs to:

_____

_____

This Book is Dedicated to:

My Spectacular Mom!

That's right, Ma. This book is for YOU!

Possibilities & Tea, Second Edition, 2019
Series: Little Books for Little Warriors Volume 1
Written and illustrated by Jessycka Drew

Copyright © 2017, 2019
All rights reserved.
MotherButterfly Books
www.motherbutterfly.com

All Rights Reserved. No part of this publication may be reproduced or transmitted in any form or by any means, electronic or mechanical, including photocopying, recording, or any information storage and retrieval systems, without permission in writing from the publisher.

Requests for permission to make copies of any part of this work should be submitted online at www.motherbutterfly.com

ISBN 978-1-9995735-1-5

www.motherbutterfly.com

laugh.learn.love

Greetings dear one,
from Jessycka Drew.
I write little books with messages to YOU!

My little books give you some help with all sorts of things that may come about.

This little book

has a message for YOU.

For when you are stuck in

Life's sticky goo!

When life gets to be a HARD thing to do...

You may feel that you've lost the YOU that is YOU!

Life can get

STICKY & TRICKY

it's true.

Anger or sadness can make you quite BLUE!

If you slip, fall, & stick into GOO,

it may be hard to see your way through.

Fear not, my dear one, for there is a way out!

That is precisely what this little book is about!

There is a way out of life's sticky goo.

A way to get back the remarkable YOU!

The secret to life is simple you see...

There are SO MANY kinds of tea, my friend...

Infinite, really! Your choices never end!

What is it about

infinite tea

that can pull you out

of your misery?

Infinite tea means
INFINITY
&
INFINITY
is exactly the key!

There is no end for you to see of the INFINITE flow of POSSIBILITY!

It flows through you & it flows through me.
So flow yourself out of that misery!

Infinity is a magical key.
Enormously big and tricky to see!

It's a forever & ever flowing sea of endless flowing POSSIBILITY.

Because YOU have the power to get YOU unstuck!

Dream & wish,

& create something new!

If you believe in

the infinitely beautiful you...

dear one, your dreams will come TRUE!

Dear one, do you know how spectacular you are? Every bit of your being, every freckle & scar?

Your worth in this world outnumbers the stars.

You are infinity. Truly you are.

Wise OWL Tea

Tips & Tricks

When you are feeling
sad, angry, or blue,
look into the mirror and
say this to YOU!

Repeat this over & over to you...
Beacause it is so amazingly true.

Ready?!
Don't be shy...
Here we go!

Trace UP and DOWN...
Breathe IN and OUT...

On the INFINITE calming Round-A-Bout.

With your finger slowly trace, breathing deep, keep the pace, until your thoughts no longer race.

UP! Breathe in deep.

DOWN we go! Breathe out slow.

Deeply breathing IN and OUT, take the Infinite Round-A-Bout!

GO TO:

motherbutterfly.com/littlewarriors
for your FREE book!

Loved this Book?

Sharing is Caring!

Please share the love by leaving a review online.

THANK YOU for helping to share our books with families around the world!

- GoodReads
- Amazon
- Indigo
- Barnes and Noble
- iBooks
- Google Play
- Kobo

laugh.learn.love
MotherButterfly.com

www.ingramcontent.com/pod-product-compliance
Lightning Source LLC
Chambersburg PA
CBHW041108070526
44583CB00002B/108